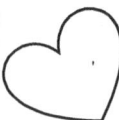

50 REASONS WHY I LOVE YOU

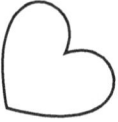

Copyright © 2020 Tatsiana
All rights reserved.
ISBN: 978-1-7322587-1-6
Book design, illustrations and cover design by Tatsiana
First Paperback Edition

Dear:_____

Here are 50 reasons why I love you

From:_____

Disclaimer: I love you for no reason!
I love you with all my heart!

♡

In this book I tried my best to express why I am so blessed and grateful to have you in my life!

♡

When I first met you...

_____
_____
_____
_____
_____

♡

I fell in love with your

_____

I love when we

_____

together

You encourage me to
_____

♡

I love that you are my
_____

You make me feel

_____

♡

I love the way you

_____

I love how

_____

you are

♡

I love that you want to

_____

with me

9

You think I'm

_____

even when I don't.

♡

You have taught me

_____
_____
_____
_____
_____

I miss you when

_____
_____
_____

I love to

_____

for you

My favorite memory of you is

_____
_____
_____
_____
_____

I believe the world needs your

_____

When you are around

_____
_____

♡

You know how to make me

_____

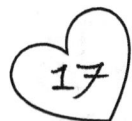

When I'm hurt, you

_____

_____

I know I can tell you
everything about

_____

because

_____
_____

♡

It is so cute when you

_____

_____

I love when you say
_____
_____

I'm proud of you for

_____
_____
_____

I love all the little things about you, like

_____
_____
_____
_____
_____

♡

You are awesome when

_____
_____
_____

I can't get over how

_____

you are

You have a great

_____

♡

I love that you

_____

for me

You are the best

___

I love to watch you

_____

You deserve

_____
_____
_____

♡

I never get tired of your

_____

I love that when we disagree

_____
_____
_____

♡

I love that you are always willing to

_____
_____

You let me

You are

_____

with me

When you laugh,

_____
_____

♡

You care deeply about

_____

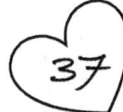

We share the same

_____

You've seen me
___

and you
___

I love your

_____

♡

Nothing makes me happier than

_____

You are a great person to

_____

♡

You make me want to
be a better

_____

♡

I can't imagine my life without

_____

♡

Thank you for being such a great

_____

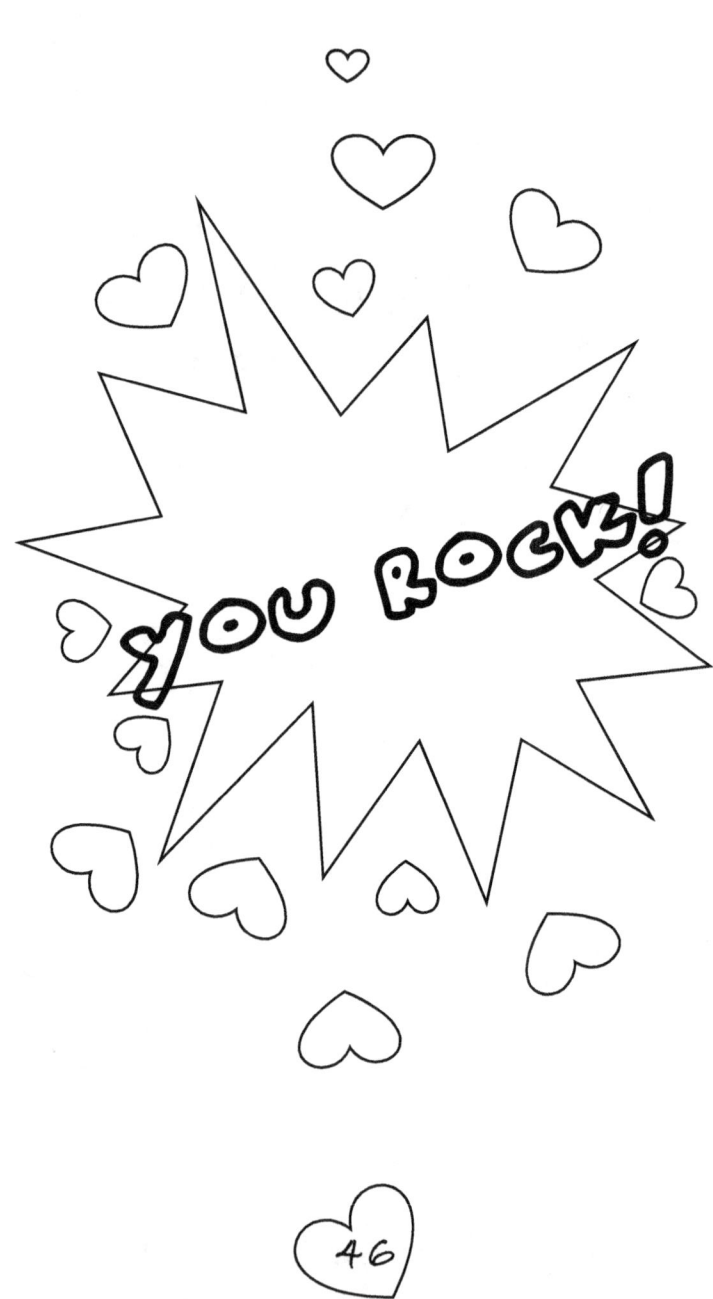

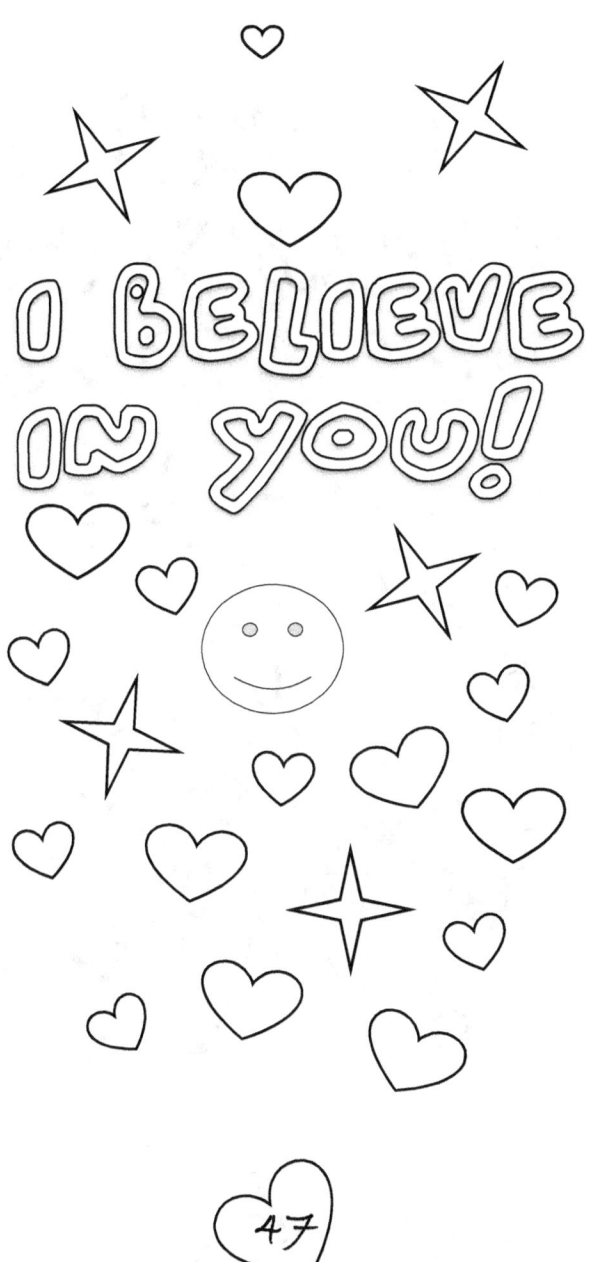

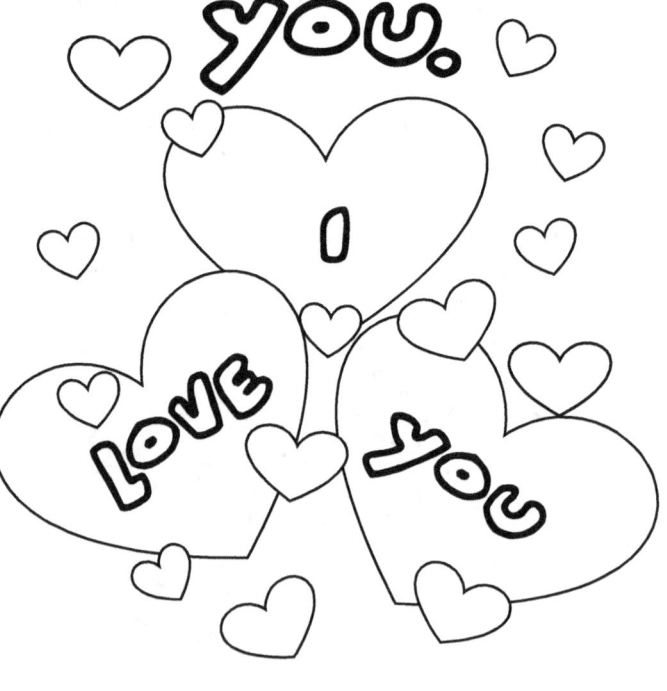

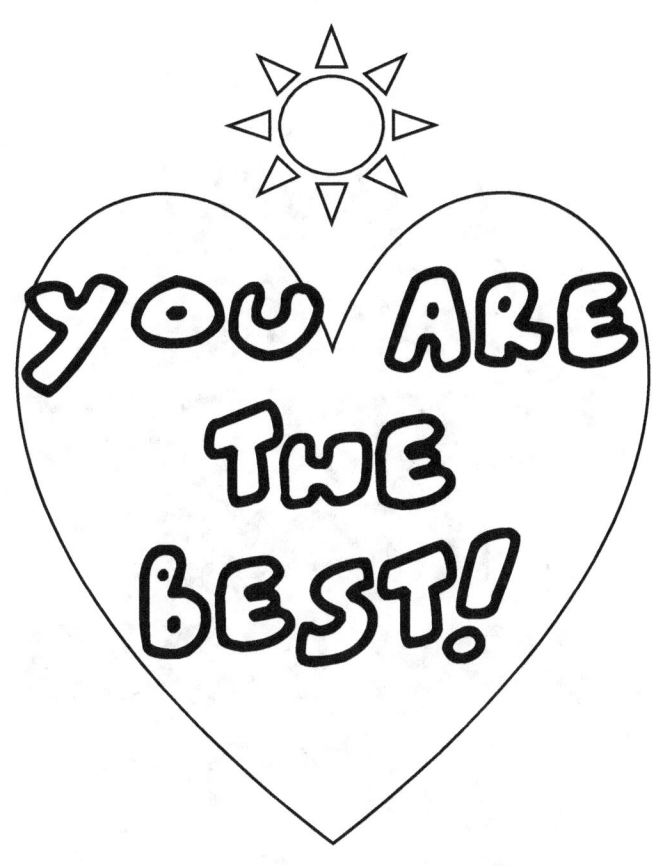

I LOVE THAT EVERY DAY I LOVE YOU MORE AND MORE...

50

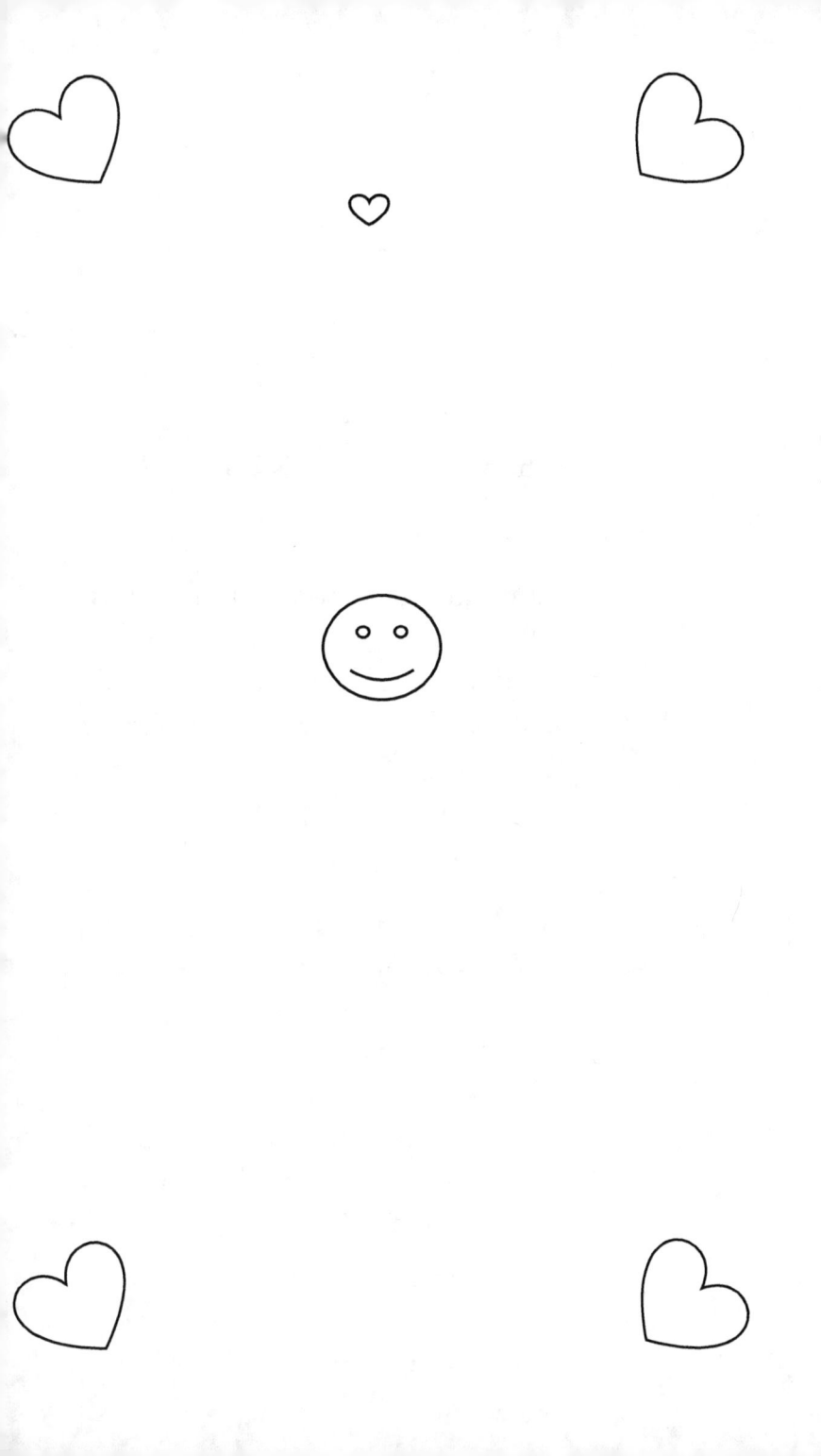

Thank you!
I hope you enjoy this book!

You can find more about Tatsiana at:
Website: www.tatsiana.us
Instagram: @tatsiana.art.inspiration
Facebook page: Tatsiana's Art & Inspiration

www.ingramcontent.com/pod-product-compliance
Lightning Source LLC
Chambersburg PA
CBHW070958240526
45469CB00017B/2452